T0368435

87
AND STILL WANDERING ABOUT

REG GREEN

AuthorHouse™
1663 Liberty Drive
Bloomington, IN 47403
www.authorhouse.com
Phone: 1 (800) 839-8640

Published by AuthorHouse 01/09/2016

ISBN: 978-1-5049-6085-4 (sc)
ISBN: 978-1-5049-6086-1 (e)

Print information available on the last page.

Any people depicted in stock imagery provided by Thinkstock are models, and such images are being used for illustrative purposes only.
Certain stock imagery © Thinkstock.

This book is printed on acid-free paper.

authorHOUSE®

Dear Reader: The infant mortality rate of newspaper articles is shocking: front page in the morning, thrown in the trash bin that night. Resuscitation is rarely a good idea – stale food warmed up. However, egotism has won – with writers it usually does – and I have given in. So, here is a collection of articles as they were written over the last few years, with just a few detailed changes here and there. I hope you will not find them too dated, localized or repetitive. If you do, remember, the recycling basket is only a throw away.

Reg Green, January 2016

Contents

Spring Comes to Long Island (Photo: Joe Woicik)

THE CAPE HORN ROUTE TO CALIFORNIA

Everyone knows what the historic crossing of the United States to California is like: Conestoga wagons baking near dried up waterholes, Okies in overheated cars, stumbling miners crazed with thirst (did you ever hear of one who wasn't?)

Having moved to California by driving from Washington DC with Maggie, my wife, in a three-day period that included some of the lowest temperatures ever recorded in the 48 states, I can vouch for a different set of impressions. Above: skies as black as night. Below: a sheet of ice covering entire states. In-between: absolutely nothing moving that positively didn't have to.

The original plan was to follow the route of the 49ers: the Platte river (the pioneers' lifeline, loosely described as a thousand miles long, one mile wide and six inches deep), then Sublette's Cut-off across the waterless desert, the Donner Pass and – to stretch a point -- Candlestick Park.

That idea was soon abandoned. The mid-West was showing temperatures close to those of the surface of the moon and Sublette's long johns were more appropriate gear than his cutoffs.

A more southerly route -- Arkansas, Oklahoma etc. – looked like a fair compromise between recklessness and timidity. But it quickly proved to be an illusion. From the start, our car was continually being forced south by road closures, like a small boat in a northerly gale.

Every time we tried to turn west, we found ourselves blocked. The whole of Tennessee was sealed, Arkansas had retreated into a new Ice Age, New Mexico was closed for the season.

Eventually, our frail craft was forced further south than any prairie schooner would have believed. Even the iconic Deep South landmarks were no protection: magnolias shivered near Billy Graham Drive, peach trees were petrified on Jimmy Carter Boulevard and winds pierced on Lee Trevino Drive. Freezing rain, not stars, fell on Alabama.

Interstates in Mississippi (home of *Cat on a Frigid Tin Roof*) were barricaded until further notice. The early morning faces in hung-over New Orleans – yes, we had to go all that far to find passable roads -- were as ashen pale as usual but this time they were covered with hoar frost too.

At each stage the car radio would relish more severe trials ahead. 'The city streets are like glass.' 'Stay home and make popcorn' or, for more mature listeners, 'Stay home in bed.' I saw new meanings in immigrants being called huddled masses.

The Texas hill country was a mess of crawling traffic; mesquite dripped with icicles near El Paso; a blizzard erupted in Arizona where the normal hazard is hot sand blocking the road.

Right on the Mexican border as we were, we began to wonder if a more southerly route still might be advisable. "How about Cape Horn?" I asked. Rain, fog and slush in Tucson, RV parks quaking in bone-chilling temperatures near Casa Grande, biting winds in Yuma.

Then across into California. It would be an untruth to say the weather changed there and then. Aged inhabitants at gas stations said they couldn't remember anything like it. Still, quite soon it became apparent that we were in a different world. Birds, the first we had seen, appeared. Not only that: they sang. We saw our first sunrise.

Instead of looking like Arctic explorers, people were dressed like – well, not like ordinary people – but like Californians. Others were working in the fields where for the last two thousand miles agriculture had seemed to be an abandoned art. Reaching Los Angeles, the sun was warm and all that frozen continent seemed as though it belonged to a different age.

I once heard a man say "Those poor people in Los Angeles. All they have is the weather." It's an absurd misconception, of course, even if stated in its milder forms. But I will say this: if that is truly all we had, it would still take an awful lot to get me out of here.

HUMBLED

I have just had the most humbling literary experience of my life. We're talking, I should point out, about a man who never goes into a grocery checkout line without a newspaper. For the pharmacy a slim volume of essays is appropriate, for the post office Shakespeare's complete works. Last-minute cramming with a physics textbook in one hand while riding a bicycle to school was routine.

Not that I read all that fast. My wife and daughter, Eleanor, who read at lightning speed, are openly contemptuous of my skills. I wear my Cheshire cat smile, however, and remind myself that, as Joseph Epstein pointed out, all writers read slowly. Like everyone else they have to absorb both content and style but in addition they are also alert for what they can steal.

I had been asked to give a reading at Pasadena's lovely central library from a book I wrote, called "The Nicholas Effect." Flattered, I turned up to find 110 other authors also had been invited. We all gave our readings separately, mine to an audience of one. (It would have been none except that a kindly lady left over from a previous session stayed out of pity.)

The resulting trauma threw me off my usual schedule and I forgot to renew the 23 books I had on loan. When I was growing up in England in the Great Depression and fines were a penny a week, it was rightly considered criminally negligent to have an overdue book – money quite simply thrown away – and I take undue pride in never, ever, running the risk.

Now, however, with fines of 25 cents a day and a truckload overdue, I approached the check-in desk with trepidation. "Can I help you?" three pleasant voices asked simultaneously. It's a feature of today's libraries that, with the precipitous decline in book reading, the staff no longer wear the perpetual frown that was the mark of their calling in former times.

It made clear that, as a borrower, you were a nuisance, likely either to be putting books back in the wrong order or even taking them away altogether. The only smile likely to appear on the librarians of yesteryear was when you owed a fine.

Now, however, they genuinely mean to assist and they have tons of goods to offer. The sectors I use most often are the oddly-named 'literature' and history, especially the beloved 810s and 940s and I reckon that -- apart from some new books that have acquired a following or one suddenly needed for the current high school essay -- if the library has a book I want it will be on the shelves.

A book before bedtime. Photo: Martin Green

And so, my bedroom looks like branch library. As it turned out the fine was $42.50, painful to both pocket and self-respect. It became bearable only when the librarian told me she once had a borrower whose fine for overdue and lost books was – I waited for it -- $350! As we know, librarians, unlike writers, are not the kind who exaggerate, so I accept it unquestioningly.

But fine or not, smile or not, I know that, of all the local government services I could get by without, the library would be the last on the list. Candles can be lit in power outages, rocks can be scrambled over if landslides block the roads, moisture can be wrung out of plants when the water runs low. But without those armfuls of books from the public library, I would have missed many of the most enlightening experiences of my life.

"Did I exceed your expectations?" librarians may soon be required to ask. "Yes, my dear," I'll say, "You certainly did."

First published in the La Cañada Valley Sun

How I Became an Addict

Last summer, I became an addict. It has caused me and my family a lot of pain and, as I hope it may be useful for others who may be tempted, I have decided to speak out.

It began as an exploration for a new sensation, as so many wrecked lives do, and I thought I would have kicked the habit at least by the fall.

But it is winter already and I am caught in the toils of something much bigger than I am. That something is the Angeles National Forest and going there every day has become as much of a compulsion as any fix.

Six months ago, when the warm weather started, I decided to get up while it was still dark, take a hike and watch the sun come up. It was wonderful and I did it again the next day.

A New Day

I'm still doing it. A lot has changed with the seasons but the essentials are still there: the perfect quiet and the sense of having that entire ring of mountains to yourself, the long, long views and the glorious moment when the sun peeps over the horizon and floods the mountain tops in a bright glow of renewal, our very own version of Omar Khayyam's:

"AWAKE! for Morning in the Bowl of Night
Has flung the Stone that puts the Stars to Flight."

I had imagined that by this time of year it would be cold and damp up there and some days it is, though even then the swirling clouds add a mysterious element to the scene. But mostly it is mild and dry even before the sun reaches you.

The hike I take most often starts just over a mile from where we live in La Cañada, a town of 25,000 people, 15 miles or so north of Los Angeles on the foothills of the bulky San Gabriel mountains. It's three miles round trip on a fire road with a not-to-be-despised but not-to-be-too-apprehensive-about elevation gain of 600 ft.

Like the weather it too seems to be part of a benign plan: unlike most mountain hikes, which save the toughest parts for the end, this one has its gentlest slope in the last few minutes.

I hope you will try it. There, at the turnaround point, the slugabeds in the whole of the Los Angeles basin, from Long Beach to the Santa Monica mountains, are stretched out before you. You will be delighted by the feeling of superiority that experience brings.

After the Fire

"Entering Burned Area. Trees may fall at any time. Potential hazards include: fallen trees, flash flooding and debris flows. Do not linger under large burned trees. Avoid this area during high winds. Be alert for falling trees."

So say the signs on some Angeles National Forest trails, like a warning on one of those commercials for a product that holds loose dentures in place but comes with the risk of a sudden loss of vision, seizures, diarrhea, fatal bleeding, and an unusual condition lasting more than four hours. And for the same reason: a heavily-lawyered bureaucracy determined that, should anything go wrong, whoever gets the blame, it's not going to be them.

Obviously, people who plan a picnic under the tallest trees during a gale in an area weakened by fire are unlikely to change their minds when they see such a sign. It is a good reminder, however, to look around at the results of the apocalyptic 2009 Station Fire, a natural disaster few of us have seen equaled.

A few days after that fire I walked down the trail that drops steeply into the Arroyo Seco from the hills above La Cañada and saw what had been profusely green canyons were now bare brown earth covered by a choking layer of grey ash and dotted with blackened tree stumps. Entire hillsides were stripped bare. Every few minutes rocks, unsupported by burned-out vegetation, slid down the valley sides.

The only signs of life were colonies of ants, busy as ever, and a few crows fighting viciously over burned scraps. Everything else had fled or died. Some clumps of trees, for some reason that was unclear, had escaped – even some individual trees among a group where all the others were dead – but overall in its aridity it was as hopeless a view of nature as I had ever seen.

Despite the scriptures, I have always thought the idea of the meek inheriting the earth was a long shot: they seem far too – well -- meek to run the whole show. Ants, however, are a much better bet to become our masters -- purposeful, tireless, organized and now, it seems, fireproof .

I knew forests recover after the most destructive fires but, looking at that dusty desert, it was hard to visualize. Now, less than five years later, all over this huge area the plants have sprung back to life with an exuberance many of us feared was beyond them.

The lifeless stumps remain but the undergrowth is more luxuriant than ever and, on some little-used side trails, impossible to force your way through.

In the Arroyo itself, the little stream -- one of whose charms is that even after months without a drop of rain, there it is, skipping along and sparkling in the sunlight -- is now so completely grown over that for long stretches you can't see it at all and only a cheerful gurgle gives it away.

Only the ants survived.

The change brings to mind the words Lorenz Hart wrote for a song that mocked Manhattan theatergoers for never getting out of the city:

"In a mountain greenery,
Where God paints the scenery ..."

Dotted among the green are clumps of brightly-colored flowers - yellow, purple, red and blue. An occasional yucca that escaped the fire is bravely displaying its delicate white foliage. Even some trees that were badly singed on one side are green with fresh leaves on the other.

Animal life has responded. You see little of it in person, so to speak, because these empty hillsides are so extensive that animals don't need to make themselves visible on forest roads but the footprints of deer and coyotes and an occasional sinewy rattlesnake trail are here again. The butterflies are back and, in favored spots, green and yellow birds "chant melody on every bush," as Shakespeare said when trying to imagine nature at its most beguiling.

I have even removed from my songbook the lines that ran insistently through my mind last fall:

> "Like a gloomy scene in Thackeray/
> All you see is mountain blackery."

The ravages are still evident all over the burned area, of course, and the problems remain formidable. But the recovery leads to a question: Do we make too much of natural disasters? The life force is so powerful, and every little component is struggling so hard to grow and reproduce, that even the tiniest opportunity offers a chance of a full recovery.

And so when friends phone from bustling New York or London and ask pointedly "What do you *do* in La Cañada?" I reply contentedly, "We're watching the grass grow."

Day One: First hesitant steps.

Day Seven: "What's the problem?"

CHILDREN, ONCE TOO ILL TO WALK ACROSS A ROOM, TAKE TO THE SKI SLOPES

High in the Swiss Alps, in the little town of Anzere, 34 children from around the world, aged 6 to 17, were preparing to ski down a 45 degree slope in a revered competition that at one time none of them could have dreamed of being in.

It was a perfect day for the climax of the World Winter Transplant Games: the Nicholas Cup, named for my seven-year old son, who was shot in an attempted carjacking while we were on a family vacation in Italy, and whose organs and corneas Maggie and I donated to seven very sick Italians, four of them teenagers.

The story caught the world's imagination and everywhere people realized, often for the first time, that when someone they love is declared brain dead, they can either bury the organs or save on average three or four desperate families from devastation. In Italy alone organ donation rates tripled in the following ten years and thousands of people there are alive who would have died.

The weather was calm and clear, the sun dazzling on the pure white snow. The course was treacherous, however, hard ice in places, difficult to dig in the edges of the skis to cut the angles round the gates and more difficult than for the usual run of skiers because, a week earlier, none of these children had ever been on skis. Until then, some – such as those from Tunisia, Hong Kong and Israel – had never seen snow. "I falled over a few times at first," one small face said proudly. "But I'm alright now."

But the real challenge was of an order of magnitude greater than all that. All of them had once been so ill that their only cure was an organ transplant: a new heart or liver, kidneys or lungs to replace the ones that were dying inside them.

Some had been desperately sick at birth – yellow or blue or a lurid shade of green. One had kidneys the size of peas. A third had to be fed through a tube and, says his mother, "for the first two years he never laughed." Some could not walk across a room without stopping for breath.

Others had lived normal lives, until felled by a virus that at first seemed no more severe than a headache. The first that one father knew of a problem was a scream in the night as one of his daughters heard her younger sister collapse on the floor and then kept her alive for forty minutes as the ambulance crew talked him through the CPR procedure.

The families have lived with a mixture of fear and unremitting care, sometimes for years. One year, just before Christmas, the parents of one of the children were told by their hospital contact that the chances of a new organ arriving in time were now so slim that the only thing he could suggest was that they should go home and draw on whatever solace they could find in the sanctity of the holidays.

Another father donated a kidney to his 2 year-old son: six years later his daughter needs a new kidney and his wife has offered to donate one of hers.

For many of these children any form of exercise, let alone a competition mixing risk with athletic agility, was physically impossible. On top of that the years of dependence could have eaten away fatally at their self-confidence.

Yet, on the day of the race, one by one the little figures appeared at the starting gate, high on the mountainside. Some came down with what the commentator charitably called "a racing snowplow" style and one or two held on to the instructors. But most tackled the course with assurance and a few with insouciance.

The winner was a Polish boy of 12, Marek Husar, a kidney recipient who hurtled down the icy slope like a champion.

The triumph, however, was collective: these are not sickly lives prolonged by an experimental medical procedure but children who, if anything, perform better than other kids because they exercise and eat more healthily and, having learned at close quarters how precious life is, are determined to make the most of it.

The competition was started 11 years ago by a liver recipient, Liz Schick, a British-born mother of two living in Switzerland who, like so many recipients, wanted to say 'thank you' to the world and has done it in an unforgettable way. As one 15-year old girl, who had a transplant when she was 2, and has been shunted between homes to wherever the appropriate medical treatment could be obtained, said afterward to her mother, "This was the best thing I ever did."

Going Where Ape Men Fear to Tread

Ever since I thrilled to a radio play about the Lost World, when I was 10, I have dreamed about going there.

Its real name is Mount Roraima. It is in Venezuela and is where Arthur Conan Doyle, when he wasn't writing about Sherlock Holmes, placed his story of a party of scientists attacked by dinosaurs and ape men in a land completely cut off from the rest of the world.

That was a hundred years ago and now you can get there without any special training or it costing the earth. My only preparation was hiking for an hour a day in the steep hills near where I live.

Roraima is the flat-topped mountain you saw in photos at school, when the teacher was explaining what a mesa is. It's entirely encircled by cliffs that shoot straight up, 1,500 feet or more, an island in the sky. In the book nothing can climb to the top and nothing can climb down – which is how Doyle's dinosaurs survived -- and that's more or less the way it is in reality.

The result: on the top is a greater proportion of unique life than almost anywhere else in the world, including a tiny black frog so primitive that it hasn't yet learned to hop but, when threatened, turns itself into a ball and rolls so rapidly off the steep rocks where it lives that it leaves its predators staring in amazement.

There are bunches of charming flowers that can't get enough nutrition from the paper-thin soil and supplement their diet by enticing insects to sip from their nectar and then murder and devour them.

The journey is, of course, infinitely easier than it was in Doyle's day – no more weeks and weeks of toiling up the Amazon and its tributaries, sloshing through snake-infested swamps and plodding across endless grasslands to get within striking distance.

From then on, however, the challenge hasn't changed much in a hundred, or even a few thousand, years -- a trek across the burning savanna, interrupted by a couple of river crossings that are fun in the December to April dry season but often become impassable without warning at other times -- which would be inconvenient if you're going toward the mountain, deadly if you're trapped trying to come back.

Then the trail rises steadily but inexorably, a gain of 2,700 feet to base camp, where grassland gives way to jungle at the foot of that monstrous vertical wall of rock, higher than the Empire State building, the top of which often disappears into the clouds. For once I'm not ashamed to say 'awesome.'

Around you is the teeming vegetation you expect of a jungle, though you are probably unprepared for the largest concentration of orchids in South America, a bewildering variety of shapes and sizes, some patterned like butterflies, some like birds, some like human lips and every color, shade and combination of the rainbow plus deathly white and deadly black.

Experience now comes to the rescue. You've been on many trails and know that, if there's a way up, putting one weary foot in front of the other eventually overcomes the highest mountain. True, you've never walked up the side of a skyscraper before but the principle is the same.

I'm there, in the red shirt, bottom right.

You scramble up a seemingly endless series of rocky staircases and gullies of bare earth, hauling yourself up by roots or branches or faith. Higher and higher you go, puffing and sliding, with occasional glimpses between your feet of the tops of trees far, far below.

Then comes a steep rock-strewn track that forces its way between the jungle and the wall, the one gap in the whole impregnable castle. So, yes, there is a route to the top, 2,700 feet above base camp, that doesn't require any technical climbing skills, and in my party, which included a plucky girl of 13, we all did it without undue problems.

On top the reward was immediate: a strange, misshapen world that leaves nothing unimaginable. The predominant color is black – black rocks, black bogs, a few black butterflies, an occasional tarantula. But, even here, there are orchids, not so flamboyant as in the totally different environment a few hundred feet below, but nevertheless making a life for themselves in one of the most demanding places on earth.

It is a climate of extremes, an unremitting struggle between the blazing sun and the drenching northeast trade winds. Changes are almost instantaneous as one or other of the elements momentarily gains the upper hand: in a few moments you go from looking at a view stretching to the far horizon to stumbling through impenetrable fog. Parched soil like a desert alternates with rock pools deep enough to bathe in and waterfalls to shower under. Although nearly on the equator, nights can be bitterly cold.

You're conscious of living very close to the edge. A tent blown down in a rainstorm, a lost compass in that rocky maze, even a sprained ankle could be serious up here. Around every corner you're relieved that you didn't meet an ape man.

The beauty of it is melodramatic too -- fiery sunsets, primeval dawns and the tension that comes from being on a spectacular natural frontier. In how many places in the world can you see dry plains thousands of feet below you in one direction and an impassable rain forest in the other? On clear nights, the full moon is bright enough to read by. And one night I saw a moonbow, the very ghost of a rainbow, caused by the moon shining on drops of rain.

With darkness falling by 6.30 pm, only sharp rocks for a seat and mist swirling everywhere, dinner – a hefty portion of meat that could be boiled baby pterodactyl – is soon over. With no fire to sit around – there's not a trace of wood -- and no soothing glass of wine, we all turn in early with, for me, the anticipated tingle of reading "The Lost World" on location.

Amazing how, after a while, the slight rustling sound caused by the wind on the tent becomes indistinguishable from what a huge curved beak might sound like, hunting for frogs' legs as an appetizer, perhaps, but ready also for an entrée of good red human meat. I've hiked amid many beautiful mountains but I can't remember one that was more satisfying to the imagination.

(First published in the Los Angeles Times)

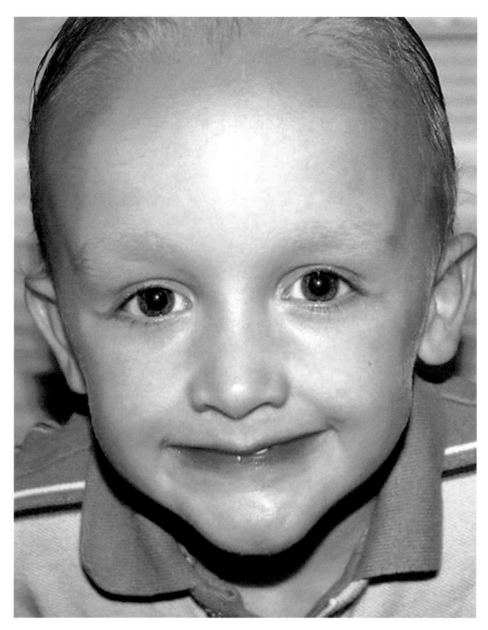

Noah Davis, Honorary Police Officer (Courtesy: the Davis family)

THE SEVEN-YEAR OLD POLICEMAN

Six-year old Noah Michael Davis of Shawnee, Kansas. wanted to be a policeman so he could make sure "everyone was safe." He didn't make it. Instead, he drowned in the family swimming pool and was declared brain dead. Although he couldn't help everyone, his family did donate his kidneys, giving two very sick people their lives back. On what would have been his seventh birthday, he was sworn in as an honorary police officer.

Noah's story will have a special place in this year's Rose Parade on January 1, which will be seen by nearly a million spectators and 20 million television viewers around the world. His portrait, made entirely of flowers and other natural materials, will travel on the Donate Life float, which each year inspires people of all ages to become organ, eye and tissue donors.

Noah is only one of the donors who died painfully young who will be honored by the float. Nearly one-third of the 81 floral donor portraits are for those aged 17 or younger. The youngest of all is Annie Rachel Ahern of Oklahoma City, whose family knew five months before she was born that she had anencephaly, which prevents normal brain development. But her parents and sisters wanted to hold and kiss her and put their cheeks against hers on her fleeting visit to the world. In the few hours she was here, Annie brought joy to the world by donating her tiny organs.

The waiting list continues to grow with more than 120,000 Americans, from infants to great-grandparents, hoping for the gift of life. It's breathtaking, isn't it, that so many of them will receive that gift from a child?

In her book on Mt. Everest, Jan Morris said an ascent should not be attempted without Frank Cooper's Oxford marmalade. I sent her this photo to let her know I'm in training.
(Photo: Martin Green)

I Contradict a Famous Writer! About Writing!! Then Have to Apologize!!!

Ms. Morris,

You have been on my conscience for some years and since, at 84, I may not have it much longer, I want to apologize to you.....

So began a letter I wrote a few months ago to Jan Morris, who I have never met but whose writing I have admired since I worked on the Guardian newspaper in England when she wrote exhilarating feature articles for the paper. I remember lapping them up in the first edition of the paper on the late-night bus going home from work.

At that time she was James Morris, formerly of the Queens Royal Lancers, later attached to the team that made the first successful ascent of Mt. Everest, scooping the world with the news. Later still he would have the most sensational sex change operation Britain has ever known, becoming Jan Morris.

I recently re-read *Heaven's Command* in which she describes how the British army, the most formidable fighting force in the world, was annihilated by hill tribesmen, including small boys, as it retreated from Afghanistan in 1842. It was as rich in imaginative insight and precision of language as I remembered it but no more so than the score of other books she has written, all of them crown jewels. As the London Daily Telegraph dutifully reported, "Recently she was named the 15th greatest British writer since the Second World War."

I was writing to her because three or four years earlier, after I saw an article of hers in the Wall St. Journal on the value of exclamation marks, I sent a letter to the editor saying that the rule in Fleet Street was that you were allowed only one a century.

As I explained to her: "I was reacting to the flood of emails I was receiving with one, two, sometimes three, exclamation marks at the end of sentences which, with the least dexterity, the writer could have made quite clear without them. As soon as I saw my letter in the paper, I regretted it or -- at least -- for not saying that in fastidious hands like yours the exclamation point has a point.

"However, for literally years after that, I *never* used one of them because, whenever I was tempted, I felt I would never be able to face you. In the last few months, I've capitulated and, if a sentence needed one, dammit, I've used it -- and I feel a lot better for it.

"So, please forgive my crassness. I hope you will go on inspiring us for many years."

I had cleared my conscience and felt prepared for death. Astonishingly, a few days later the telephone rang and a voice said, "It's Jan Morris" and it was! She was calling from her home in Wales.

We chatted, a vibrant amused voice at her end, words-tumbling-over-each-other in don't-waste-a-moment-responses at mine and once again I had been reminded that the genuine greats are as easy to approach as you and I are.

I had learned this lesson many years before when a friend was lodging with the legendary Professor R.H. Tawney, whose works shaped my entire view of economics as a young student. One day I called the house to speak to the friend and a reedy ancient voice answered. It was him!! It was he!!! I stumbled to find the words to tell this Olympian of my debt to him and, as I did, his barely-alive but urgent voice summed up the moment. "The kettle's boiled dry," he cried and put the phone down. He died soon afterward and I vowed never again, if there is any likelihood that this might be the last time, to miss the opportunity of letting someone know how I feel about them.

So, when Christopher Hitchens was dying in a way too sublime to sully by ill-considered chatter, I wrote to his publisher who agreed to give him a note from me to show him one unlikely way that his writings would live on. I wrote that I had brought to the attention of a teacher at my children's high school a limerick he quoted in one of his books. The teacher liked it so much that it is now part of the history curriculum there. It ran as follows:

There was an old bastard called Lenin

Who did one or two million men in.

That's a lot of men to have done in

But, where he did one in,

That old bastard Stalin did ten in.

I cling to the hope that the prospect of generations of high school students learning to summarize Bolshevism in this way might have acted as a little candle for him as the darkness closed in.

The Treeless Forest

Have you noticed that in La Cañada the trees stop where the national forest begins? Look down sometime from the Cherry Canyon trail on the south side of the valley. Although there is not an empty lot to be seen, trees dominate the view.

Their variety is equally surprising, even for someone who has never hugged a tree in his life. On the one hand, are the dark groves of deodars that put me in mind of the phantom wood in Disney's "Snow White" and, at the other end of the cultural scale, the orderly rows of cypress trees more suited to classical Rome.

They call this a forest?

Then there are the deciduous trees, discreetly hidden among the prevailing evergreens for most of the year -- but suddenly bursting out in startling splotches of gold and red in the fall -- and the delicate blue jacaranda adding a hint of tropical jungle to city streets in the spring.

Highways in some favored parts of the world advertise themselves as Palm to Pine and in an hour or two you make that dramatic transition. We have one like that here. In the center of town the road going into the mountains is signed Palmdale 40 miles, Big Pines 56.

But you don't need to travel even that distance. In the yard of our house, just a few feet from each other, there are towering pines and cactus, sycamore, olive and a palm tree so ugly I can't bear to look at it. That's multiculture for you.

But I forgot, you are still in Cherry Canyon. So raise your eyes a little higher than the unnatural green of the country club's golf course and what do you see? Shrubs, grass, bare slopes and a handful of trees. Welcome to the Angeles National Forest. If you told Robin Hood this was a forest he would fetch you a blow with his quarterstaff.

But for many of us this is just what we want: a few dirt roads and trails through thick low-lying vegetation that allows views to the horizon but defies any tidying up, mountain slopes too steep for a developer and water that, unlike the careful irrigation lower down, more often comes in dramatic downpours and then disappears as quickly as it started. If you haven't done it already, I hope you will take a drive someday and stroll alongside the California aqueduct and marvel that this stream, narrow enough for a child to throw a rock across, is one of the feats of engineering that have transformed our near-desert into one of the most dynamic regions on earth. Amazing – don't you think? – that the line between dearth and abundance, wasteland and civilization, is that flimsy.

A Full Moon, a Lonely Road and a Parked Car

At three o'clock one recent Sunday morning, somewhere in the San Francisco Bay area, I was sitting in a van alone with Ana, a woman more than 40 years younger than I am on a deserted road under a full moon. This is what Shakespeare had in mind when he talked of the stuff that dreams are made on and what the chief of police has other names for.

Would they have believed us, I wondered, if we'd told them that I, a 78-year-old man, was there because I had just finished a solitary six-mile walk along this black country road lit only by the moon and with just the rustle of an occasional small animal in the undergrowth to break the silence? And that it was part of a 128-mile relay race aimed at bringing attention to people who need an organ transplant?

Perhaps they would, because my companion, 34-year-old Ana Stenzel, had rigged up on one side of her a curtain rod holding up a tube that was giving her medications intravenously and on the other had a tank, dangerously low on oxygen, that was keeping her breathing.

I owed my precarious situation to an annual 199-mile relay run from Calistoga to Santa Cruz, which starts one morning, goes through the night and finishes the next afternoon, and is designed to remind people of the thousands of lives lost in the United States every year through the acute shortage of donated organs. The relay walk is the shorter, less heroic, but still testing, version over most of the same course.

It is testing not simply because it goes on all night and over the Santa Cruz Mountains, but also because, although some participants are strong walkers, many others have had serious health problems and some have been at death's door.

Of the 12 people on my walking team, one had received a new pair of lungs only 10 months before, another was a grandmother who has had a liver transplant and a third had donated one of her kidneys to her husband, who was also on the team.

Two others, though not hit directly by illness, were parents of children who had suffered from cystic fibrosis since birth, the killer that attacks the lungs and doubles up its victims in coughing spasms during the day and wakes them at night in a panic. And then there was me, who at my age should have been in bed hours earlier after a supper of bread, with the crust cut off, dipped in warm milk.

In the van were various reminders of mortality, including a wheelchair and enough pills to keep CVS in business for a month. I remember the little tremor that ran through me when I was told that, when it was my turn to walk my two segments of five and six miles, I needed to wear a bib with my medications listed on it. Just in case.

Ana Stenzel, able to breathe freely for the first time in her life after receiving a fresh pair of lungs from a stranger, has just climbed Half Dome in Yosemite National Park, a 17-mile roundtrip and a rise of 5,000 ft. Like most recipients she never ceased to think about her donor and his family. (Photo by Ana's father, Reiner Stenzel, who climbed with her.)

All our team knew people who had died on the transplant list, that agonizing wait that can go on for years.

In most cases, a transplant converts a sickly, frightening and restricted life into a wholesome and healthy one almost overnight. It does not guarantee plain sailing, however. Ana herself, who received new lungs in 2000 had organized the team and set her heart on competing. But transplanted lungs are particularly susceptible to rejection and she had been hit so hard in the days before the race that she was put on the list for a second transplant.

People who have endured sickness since birth often have remarkable strength and independence, however. I will never forget seeing her, still hooked up to her oxygen tank, pushing her own wheelchair across the sands at Santa Cruz. A few months later, she received a new pair of lungs and soon after that, gratefully and happily, married her faithful lover, Trent.

But in 2013 the body that had withstood and achieved so much gave out and Ana, just 41 years old, died. The only consolation her army of devotees has is knowing that her grace and courage will stay with them all their lives.

Footnote: Ana had an identical twin, Isa, who also had cystic fibrosis from birth and suffered the same excruciating symptoms and also forced herself to swim and hike vigorously. She also earned a master's degree at Berkeley, also had two transplants and also married her own devoted man, Andrew.

Not satisfied with all that, she has learned a demanding new skill for her lungs to remind herself every day of what a transformation those two transplants were: she plays the bagpipes. "I feel my transplant was a form of resurrection," she says. "I want to be worthy of it."

The cloud cover that stretches to the ocean can't get any further inland.

A Gloomy Day – But Only for Mortals

The recent change in temperature from tropical to Arctic – you'll forgive the slight hyperbole, I hope – and the resulting fifty shades of grey enveloping our city have cast a gloom on many of us. Ira Gershwin had the same response to a foggy day in London:

"I viewed the morning with alarm
The British Museum had lost its charm."

From any nearby height you can see the low-lying grey cloud stretching unbroken, from one end of the Los Angeles Basin to the other, and covering all its teeming millions. "What a crummy day" they say to themselves. Or, if so minded:

"With alarm I viewed the morn.
Trader Joe's looked quite forlorn."

But all this dullness is just for mortals. Up in the mountains, just minutes away, the gods are enjoying another perfect day.

And all of it is open to any lesser being who goes up there who does not intend to steal fire – or, more precisely, who does not light a fire outside a 'designated location' -- or become too friendly with any passing goddesses.

The transition is not gradual, not a slow lightening of the gloom on the climb through the mountains. Instead, the veil is simply ripped apart and the sunshine floods in. Black and white to Technicolor, Kansas to Oz, in a couple of hundred yards.

On the Hoyt Trail, where I hiked last Sunday and which starts at the 3,000 ft. marker, you are already looking down, not up, at that grey wet blanket. I saw only one other hiker and was a bit resentful at even this degree of intrusion. Marlon Brando once told me that just before dawn in Times Square it is so quiet you can hear your own footsteps. That is true here too. (He also said it to everyone else who saw "Guys and Dolls.")

The cloud has been unusually widespread in recent days. Normally it creeps up the valleys from Glendale and Pasadena but fast losing strength as it is forced to climb the foothills. A mile or two further into the mountains only a few wisps remain, marking the last visible vestiges of oceanic influence. From here on, going north, the land rules until you get to the Arctic Ocean. So, yes, you are right at the edge of a notable frontier.

The other day, watching the little grey cells petering out on the San Raphael hills, I was reminded of a once well-known book, called "Christ Stopped at Eboli," whose title was a saying in the deep south of Italy, meaning that Christianity, seeping all over Europe from the famous cities on the coasts and plains, never managed to climb over the mountains behind the ancient town of Eboli and overcome the primitive beliefs of people further inland.

May I offer for the next Chamber of Commerce brochure that proclaims the merits of our sunny city another slight hyperbole? "The Fog Stops at La Cañada."

(First published in the La Cañada Valley Sun)

Organ Donation Leaps Over the World's Biggest Barrier

I have just spent a week in the company of a man whose experiences throw a fresh light on the Israeli-Palestine conflict. He is Ismael Khatib, the 46-year-old father of Ahmed, a 10-year old boy who was shot six years ago, in the tense West bank city of Jenin, by an Israeli soldier who, on a day of rioting, saw him among a group of other boys holding what looked like an automatic rifle. It turned out to be a plastic model.

Ahmed was taken to the Rambam hospital in Haifi where he was declared brain dead. The doctors then did what their counterparts in hospitals all over the world now do routinely. They asked Ismael and his wife, Abla, if they would donate their son's organs to whoever was at the top of the waiting list, which is compiled regardless of race or religion.

The Khatibs consulted their religious leaders -- who signaled their agreement -- and their donation leapt what is probably the most bitterly-divisive barrier in the world, Ahmed's organs going to six Israelis, all of them small children, four of them Jews.

I met Ismael when we were together on a tour of Eastern Canada which included talks with Muslim, Jewish and Christian communities. It was arranged by George Marcello of Toronto, who has had two liver transplants and has walked across Canada carrying a torch – subsequently blessed by Pope John Paul II -- to tell everyone who will listen that tens of thousands of people around the world die every year because of the shortage of donated organs. George, lion-hearted in determination and achievement, is one of those remarkable recipients who cannot rest until they have paid back everything they can think of to a world that has shown them such unexpected selflessness.

In the hate-filled atmosphere of the Palestinian question, where every action is weighed by the committed on both sides to see what propaganda can be wrested from it, the implications of saying 'yes' to organ donation are profoundly ambivalent.

Some Palestinians are embittered about Ahmed's organs going to Jews. Many others are using the donation quite cynically as a way of claiming a moral ascendancy over their enemies and advancing their cause in its wake. Given the intensity of the conflict, everyone involved can be presumed to have mixed emotions.

But what is perfectly clear is that to take the organs of a dead person, put them in the bodies of several others who are dying and out of that produce a crop of healthy lives is a triumph for humanity.

Yael Gladstone, seen here at Niagara Falls, is the sister of Yoni Jesner, a Jewish pre-medical student from Glasgow who was killed when a Palestinian suicide bomber blew up the bus he was traveling on when visiting Tel Aviv. Next to her is Khaled Khatib from the Palestinian town of Jenin, whose ten-year old brother, Ahmed, was shot by an Israeli soldier who thought the plastic replica of an assault gun he was holding was real. Both families donated their son's organs. One of Yoni's kidneys went to a seven-year old Palestinian girl. Six of Ahmed's organs went to young Israeli children, four of them Jews. Yael and Khaled are holding the Torch of Life that George Marcello, a Canadian who has had two liver transplants, has single-handedly made an international symbol of the power of organ donation to bridge even the world's most bitter divisions. He has walked across Canada carrying it, showing it in hundreds of towns and villages, and took it to Rome, where Pope John Paul II blessed it.

We can hope too that transplantation, with its ability to scrupulously avoid discrimination, will also be a stepping stone in bringing the whole world a little closer together. Since meeting Ismael I often think of Yoni Jesner, a 19-year-old Scottish Jew, who was killed by a suicide bomber in Tel Aviv in 2002 and one of whose kidneys went to a seven-year-old Palestinian girl.

The closing event on our tour added one more dimension, a talk to the governing council of an aboriginal community, the kind of society that from time immemorial has believed that tampering with the body is taboo. Now, it turns out, almost all of them have signed donor cards. For them also a medical miracle has modified the beliefs of all those accumulated generations and life has trumped death.

Home Town: 76 Years Later

A few years ago I went back to visit the town where I was born, Accrington, (population 40,000) in the north of England, at that time a cotton spinning town, a community that appears in the history books in the 12th century but exploded into importance only in the 19th century as one of the places that led the industrial revolution, changing the world more radically than it had ever been changed before -- and then in the 20th resumed its age-old position of moderate obscurity.

I lived here until I was 10 and have been back only half a dozen times since then. With the death of the cotton mills, the local economy has again changed drastically but what is amazing to me is how many of its features are largely the same as they were, including both houses where we lived.

I was pleased to see that the view from Westwood Street, where we lived when I was born in 1929, still includes the viaduct that steam trains used to puff across thrillingly on their way to the seaside town of Blackpool, 35 miles away, and other far-off places. Avenue Parade, where our other house was, also looked much as it did, except that there was almost no place to park. In the 1930s I'm guessing there were times when not one car was parked on that quarter-of-a-mile-long street.

The house where we lived in 1939(!) looks just as it did then. ©Alexander P. Kapp

At the top of the street was the town's hill, the Coppice, my introduction to the headiness of mountains. At one time, as its name indicates, it was well wooded but when I was growing up it I remember it as almost completely bare, the victim I imagine of industry's voracious appetite for fuel before the coal era. Now it is full of trees again, the result of a post-World War II municipal environmental project.

As I wandered along a woman in her fifties came striding purposefully toward me. "She'll know," I thought. "Excuse me. Can you tell me when these trees were planted?" I asked. "Oh, they've been here forever," she said. And, of course, for her they had.

I saw a 'for sale' sign on a house close to ours and asked a passerby what it was likely to sell for. "Oh, about 110,000 pounds," he said. When we were there almost no one owned a house. I calculate that to pay 110,000 pounds in rent, we could have lived there roughly four thousand years.

It was a holiday at Peel Park primary school so I couldn't go in but little had altered on the outside – the same sturdy building which, like all civic buildings in the town, plainly said 'We will do what is expected of us but we don't stand for any nonsense. Behave yourself.'

I went into the small street next to it where, because there was no playing field, we had our version of a sports day. Even that modest place conjured up a precious memory of my last year at the school.

In each heat there were only two runners because we had to keep on the sidewalk. In the 50-yard dash I raced against a boy called Hubert, a friend normally, but that day an intense rival. It ended in a dead heat and we had to run again.

This time through the excitement I heard Miss Thorpe – voluptuous Miss Thorpe – shouting "Come on, Reggie. Come on." I don't remember who won. What did it matter? It was me she loved.

But what I remember most about those far-off days is the spirit of self-reliance that enveloped everyone. People did what they could for themselves, helped their neighbors without asking questions and, when something bad came along, instinctively tried to make the best of it without making a fuss.

Despite the easily-mocked small-town feel of the pleasures and aspirations that dominated my early days, I'm grateful for those sturdy values. I continually fail to live up to them (you too?) but they are always in my mind and that's not a bad place to start.

A Day That Starts with a Bucketful of Water in the Face

I've just come back from a hair-raising day of rafting on the Middle Fork of the American River, billed as "one of California's premier adventures." And it is: 18 miles of it in an isolated 2000 ft.-deep canyon in the gold country, dotted with class III and IV rapids – the latter defined as "difficult to very difficult, long turbulent rapids with powerful waves and holes and many obstacles requiring precise maneuvering."

This is us: a lazy day on the river (Photo: Hotshot Imaging Inc.)

It's true that thousands of people do these trips every year so it isn't pioneering. The remarkable thing for me, however, is that I have any hair to raise. I'm 81, have an artificial heart valve and last fall, while in Northern California, had an emergency operation that took out part of my insides. But, though I left my heart in San Francisco and half my colon in Sacramento, I don't want the rest of me to be washed up on a sandbank for future boatloads to shudder at.

I got into this in much the same way you get into a Class IV rapid: a light-hearted acceptance of a suggestion while the idea was no more than a ripple on the surface, a growing tremor as the day approached and the reality sank in – no, don't say sank – as the reality dawned, that this wasn't going to be like the water chute at a theme park and the recognition, as I put on my safety helmet, that the whole plan was based on a false assumption of invulnerability. Why, I asked myself, is one of these rapids called "Last Chance"?

Within moments you are into the first big one: the front of the raft goes down and undulates violently, a bucketful of cold water hits you full in the face, your perch on the edge of the raft, which felt precarious from the start, now seems suicidal and you vow that if you survive you will never be mean to anyone again.

Time and again after that you see the water gathering speed, rippling up to a boil, hurtling toward a crevasse between massive boulders, then -- whoosh -- a fresh consignment of cold water knocks the breath out of you, the raft twists and turns and drops wildly into a hole. All the while you are working like a demon, praying you aren't forward paddling while everyone else is going backward. In the quiet sections you often hear a distant roar ahead as of enemy armies gathering.

At one point the river races madly through a narrow tunnel blasted by gold miners – "there's nothing like it anywhere else in rafting" says the blurb (surely that can't be good) -- the deathly white water even more threatening in the half-light. "If you fall out of the boat in this section roll yourself into a ball and just go with the flow," our guide said. Where else would you go?

Conditions change in the twinkling of an eye. Soaked from head to foot one minute, you are drying off in 95 degree heat the next and drenched again a minute later. After catapulting over the top of a malevolent rock, with all thoughts of exerting any control over your destiny long gone, your boat can land in a limpid pool and you wonder what all the fuss was about.

One stretch is so calm that we all waded alongside the boat and, from time to time, the more adventurous jumped out to float over the more forgiving rapids. At the end of the day you are pleasantly tired but not worn out and, of course, exhilarated by the adventure and the beauty of the surroundings. I've hiked along the American River several times but never before had any real understanding of what the 49-ers went through. Now, I think, every one of them deserved a pot of gold.

(First published in the Los Angeles Times)

The Bravest Christmas Gift of All

On December 24, 2009, 22-year old Cora Brittany Hill of Orlando, Florida, voluntarily gave the ultimate Christmas gift: her own life. Exactly two years earlier – Christmas Eve 2007 – she had received the only possible cure for the disease that was killing her, cystic fibrosis, which so completely destroys the lungs that every breath has to be forced in and out and is eventually fatal. The cure: a new pair of lungs, donated by the family of a stranger who had just died.

But transplants, though they have an impressively high rate of success, are not infallible. In time the new lungs failed and Cora, in chronic pain and too weak for another transplant, could be sustained only on a ventilator.

Calmly, but definitively, she told her family she wanted to be taken off life support and donate her kidneys in time for Christmas to whomever on the waiting list needed them most. As her mother, Dee, sublimely put it, "Two families knew the joy of new life …..on the night that miracles happen," just as her own family had experienced the same exultation two years before.

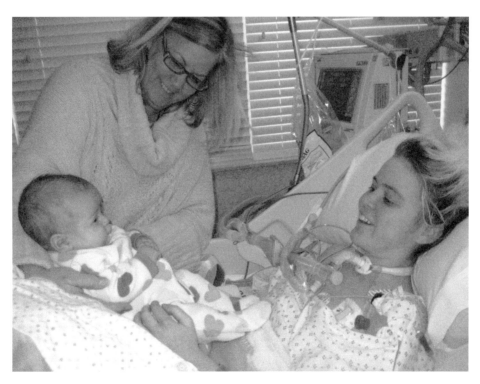

Cora holds Taylor, the daughter of a friend, two days before she was taken off life support at her own request. Her mother, Dee (who is in the photo) calls this Cora's last smile.
(Courtesy of the Hill family.)

Maquis (well, maquis-like) country

Now It Can Be Told: I Was a Maquisard

For the first time I am revealing to friends that I am a maquisard. They are amazed.

During the German occupation of France in World War II, the maquisard, some of them very young, earned a reputation as implacable resistance fighters.

They took over whole areas of near-wilderness, sallying out to sabotage railroad lines or military equipment, then disappearing back into their natural fortress. They emerged undefeated to link up with the invading allies in 1944. I was 15 years old and these were stirring times.

They — or perhaps I should say we — take our name from the vegetation of south-eastern France, the maquis, evergreen scrub growing thickly enough to make any movement off the trails difficult or impossible but, with few trees to impede the view, allowing lookouts to spot an enemy miles away. As it is also mountainous, with steep slopes and ravines, it is ideal terrain for guerrillas opposing formations of regular troops.

How did I come to be a maquisard? Why, simply by taking a daily hike there. In Los Angeles, a replica of south-eastern France is on the doorstep: the Angeles National Forest. Like its counterpart, the climate is dry and sunny, the vegetation – though here called chaparral -- stunted and tough, the mountains challenging. Views in the clear air are long and spectacular.

Strictly speaking, I should call myself a "chaparralard," but my friends would be much less impressed.

First published in the La Cañada Valley Sun

Angeles Crest Highway snakes up (and up), the power line goes straight through and I go the easy way by helicopter, thanks to the project manager, who saw my childish interest in all they were doing.

Powering Across the Mountains

Crews are just finishing adding new power lines into the Gould Mesa substation 15 miles or so north of Los Angeles, which carry twice as much capacity as the existing lines. The current, which will go into the California grid comes from Kern County, where the electricity is generated mainly by windmills.

In this busy scene, helicopters land men on the tops of the new 200 ft. transmission towers. Linemen stand on the skips of other helicopters, hovering hundreds of feet over canyons, and attach colored marker balls, 3 ft. or more in diameter, to the new cable to warn off low-flying planes. Hefty vehicles lift, pull, push, carry, dig holes and fill them in.

Other helicopters carry a 3/8 inch rope which is placed over pulleys high up on the towers. This is then attached to a wire and it in turn to the 2¼ inch diameter cable that carries the current. The whole immense line, on average 1,000 ft., is then winched up, foot after foot, by massive vehicles, called (what would you expect?) pullers. That done, the job moves on to the next tower, then the next and the one after that for a total of 170 miles.

Everything is on a huge scale. On sites high in the mountains, hooks and chains, almost too heavy to lift, outsized clasps, thick rope, ladders and pulleys lie in neat piles. The smallest component I could find of any kind was a nut and bolt 2 1/2 inches long, weighing half a pound. A tool bag warns that its load limit is 100 lb. A truck is labeled '60,000 lb. puller.'

To reach Gould Mesa the cable has had to cross the whole width of the San Gabriel mountains, a wilderness of deep valleys, totally uninhabited and subject to strong winds, torrential rain, scorching temperatures, crumbly soil, wildfires and virtually impenetrable vegetation. This is not what people think of when you tell them you live in Southern California.

Each tower has to be treated individually. Some stand on the edge of cliffs where the weight of the cable is several times as heavy as on the flat. The cables have to be taut enough so that they do not flap together in a storm but not so tight that the strain on the structures is too great. The very last swing of the cable from the Mt. Lukens fire road into the substation is a vertical drop of nearly a thousand feet.

In this giant's world, safety is obviously a supreme priority for both Southern California Edison and PAR Electrical, the contractors for this segment of the Tehachapi project, as it is called. Hiking on a fire road one day this week I met Tony Aguilera, a young man who works for PAR and is planning to be a lineman, a job that requires 7,000 hours of on-the-job training plus classroom work spread over four years.

That day one of his jobs was to make sure no one strayed along this lonely road at a time when work might be going on overhead that could possibly present some danger. This is a hike I have done a thousand times. In all those miles I have never seen more than three people at a time and generally there is no one. I would have bet a thousand to one I would never meet a traffic controller on it.

But safety is compatible with politeness, it seems. At the beginning of a dirt road to one of the busiest sites is the most decorous sign I have ever seen in a long lifetime of trespassing. "Warning. Construction Zone Ahead. Unauthorized Entry Discouraged." How nice. I have to say I wasn't discouraged but I did make sure to be extra careful.

First published in the La Cañada Valley Sun

Child, Killed at Random, Gives Sight to Others

When Roxanna Green takes her place in the upcoming Rose Parade, she will be among people who share a unique blend of anguish and inspiration. Roxanna is the mother of Christina-Taylor Green, a 9-year-old girl who was killed when a gunman fired into the crowd at an outdoor meeting for Congresswoman Gabrielle Giffords in Tucson.

There has been no shortage of anguish. Roxanna remembers, as in a nightmare, her daughter covered with a sheet and she, beside her, kissing her face and stroking her feet, willing her to live.

But, even as she and her husband, John, grappled with the enormity of their loss, they found the strength to make a decision to donate her corneas, restoring the sight of two people for whom there was no other cure.

The child, born on one day of indiscriminate killing, September 11, 2001 – '9/11' – and dying on another, gave the nation a reason to believe that selflessness can overcome senselessness.

Yet the loss was profound. Christina-Taylor balanced good works with good grades and was the only girl on her Little League team, perhaps not surprisingly, as her father is a scout for the Los Angeles Dodgers.

In the parade Roxanna will be on the Donate Life America float with people whose lives, though superficially very different, have much in common with hers.

Mary Ellen Decker who, when her 21-year-old son Seth committed suicide, had the fortitude to donate his organs, will be there and Janice Langbehn, whose 39-year-old life partner, Lisa Marie Pond, died of an aneurysm but who was not allowed to see her in her final hours because they were not married, leading to a directive from President Obama permitting gay and lesbian family members access to their hospitalized partners.

They will be joined by Arnold Perez, a 46-year-old screenprinter from Guatemala, who says he had never heard of transplantation until he and his wife, Eva, were asked if they would donate the organs of their 6-year-old son, Hernán, who crashed into a tree when, excited by snow on the mountains near Los Angeles, he impatiently jumped on his sled before they could stop him. When they received a letter telling them about the recipients, they both cried, Arnold remembers.

Roxanna's family will find another kind of kinship with the recipients on the float, seeing living proof of the good they themselves did. One of them, Kara Thio, was born without a bile duct and her parents learned she would need to grow to 15 lbs. before the local hospital could operate, a weight she could never reach. Instead of giving up, they searched until the California Pacific Medical Center in San Francisco undertook to try and, after a 15-hour operation, transplanted a liver into the 8-month-old, 11 lb. baby.

Christina -Taylor Green, with her mother, Roxanna (Courtesy of the Green family)

Another, Emily Fennell, received one of the first hand transplants in the United States earlier this year and after a few months is so used to it that she can scarcely remember when she had a hook where her right hand used to be.

The rapidly-developing techniques can surprise even those who know this field well. When Max Zapata donated a kidney to a total stranger, the brother of that stranger gave one of his to another stranger, whose wife gave one of hers, continuing a chain until 10 people, from California to New York, became free of the dialysis machines that until then had ruled their life.

With the roller-coaster events that every one of these people has faced, all of them will have a turmoil of emotions as they pass by the cheering crowds. In her case Roxanna will no doubt think of the mother who brought her small son to see her to say that, made fun of by the other kids, he sat alone at the back of the school bus for two weeks until a new pal came to sit with him: Christina-Taylor.

This is what's left of the Plantation

The Magic Wood

Today, early August, I heard a sound that I have not heard in months and didn't expect to hear for a few more: rain. But not just rain — rain falling on a million leaves.

On the city streets it was dull and dreary. Even the usual Sunday morning motorcycle screeches were muted. But a few minutes away, it was invigorating. I had so far forgotten the sound of rain on all those trees, a mysterious swish that comes from every side that, when it started I looked up to see if a strong wind had sprung up. (Another wonderful feeling, that, walking through a dense forest, calm and quiet, while a gale lashes the tops of the trees way above your head.)

It didn't last long and, for a place that takes the full brunt of moisture-laden bags of cloud coming in from the ocean every winter, it was derisory. But you could imagine every parched plant and insect — and firefighter too for that matter — breathing a sigh of relief.

After all these years, I'm still amazed that so much life can endure, proliferate even, in so testing a place. The vegetation is so dense that, for any walking, other than the shortest distance, it is a total barrier. Every now and again even in the middle of the hard-packed trail, where a little soil has accumulated, a few tiny yellow flowers were growing today and one beauty, startlingly white with a dash of purple at the edge of each minute leaf. A few new green leaves were sprouting among the chaparral too, bright and fresh against the somber colors around them.

At one point, I noticed newly trampled brown grass on a side trail where animals had found something and, following it, came across a tall bush weighed down on every branch with large clusters of blueberries, a little touch of paradise for dry throats -- not so succulent as those sold at Gelson's, I must admit, but not at its daunting prices either.

There used to be a dense wood of pine trees on this hike, known locally as the Plantation, that at dusk was like entering one of Grimm's fairy tales and which I was always thankful to emerge from without having been turned to stone.

Now that spellbinding wood is a wreck of blackened stumps and bare branches, caused by the infamous Station fire five years ago. Yet even on a few of these apparently lifeless hulks a lonely cone can be seen clinging to life and all around, thick and luxuriant, undergrowth is springing up in a profusion undreamed of before.

"Hope springs eternal in the human breast," says Alexander Pope. And in every seed too, it seems.

Tread carefully, that water is cold. Featherbed Moss in the Peak District of Northern England. Photo by Dave Dunford, Creative Commons.

Sloshing Through Bogland

As I go out walking in Southern California on these summer days across bone-dry land, pictures come into my mind of my hikes while growing up in the North of England, where rain not only comes with the territory but *is* the territory: underfoot, overhead and all around.

I went back earlier this year, half-wondering if the cold, the drenching downpours and the southwesterly gales were the imaginings of an old-timer anxious to prove to himself that the young sissies of today don't know how tough you had to be in those heroic times.

I parked the car at the top of a pass on the Pennine Hills, part of a chain that runs like a backbone north and south from the middle of England into Scotland. The land to the east is wet and windy, to the west wetter and windier. It was less than 2,000 ft. high, about the same as where I live in La Cañada, but is the stuff that heroes are made of.

I tried to get out of the car but the wind was too fierce. Every time I got the door open a crack and put a leg out the door slammed against it.

In the end I gave up, made a U-turn and parked on the other side of the road, the wind behind me. This time the door was torn so fiercely from my hand that I thought it would fly away and wondered briefly if the car company would accept my story that I had rented it from them with only three doors.

I wrestled it shut and started out on a trail against the unrelenting headwind in country known as featherbed moss: a scene of unsurpassed bleakness, miles of deep and often soggy black turf, unrelieved by a single tree, and cut up into uncountable steep-sided gullies, some deep as anti-tank trenches, and often with a layer of arctic water at the bottom.

I feel sure John Milton hiked here while writing "Paradise Lost," which, in view of his frailty and blindness, is indisputably heroic. I surmise this because it exactly fits his description of one corner of hell: "Fens, bogs, dens and shades of death."

In this section, the authorities have laid a trail of large flat stones to relieve the many hikers who come this way, mostly on weekends. ("Sissies!" I thought.) Midweek with a 360 degree view there was not a living creature in sight.

Night was not far distant. So with the car just dimly visible on the horizon, it seemed prudent to turn back. But now, with the wind behind me, instead of fighting for every step, I hurtled along at the mercy of the elements, like the Wicked Witch of the Southwest.

Safely back in the driver's seat in no time (the driver's seat! What wonderful expression. In charge of my own body again!) I took one last lingering look. As Lord Tennyson would have put it, if the Light Brigade had mounted its charge up here: black bogs to the right of me, black bogs to the left of me. There is certainly a grandeur about its desolation and that heady feeling of being on top of the world.

"In the old days," I thought (or, I probably thought 'In the olde days') "we would have walked from here to the nearest village, caught a train, then a bus and arrived home, in clothes that were still drying out, two hours later."

Did we really enjoy it? Oh, yes. Why else from Monday morning on would we have been working on plans to repeat the dose the following Sunday? And, on this day too, despite the griping, I had to agree: it was exhilarating.

One caveat: like everyone else in Southern California, I'm begging for rain but I have to add, like the choirboy who prayed for virtue: "But, please, not too much of it."

First published in the La Cañada Valley Sun

Indian Organ Recipients Break the Barrier

Six years ago, America's Chris Klug, world champion snowboarder, was fighting for his life. His liver was so diseased that it could not be repaired. At 33 he looked like a yellow and haggard old man.

He was saved when someone unknown to him was declared brain dead and whose family donated the organs. The liver went to Klug and two years later in a sport that places inordinate demands on the body – strength, stamina and coordination -- he took the bronze medal in the 2002 Olympics. Every year tens of thousands of other lives around the world are saved or freed from pain by similar decisions.

In India, by contrast, which I visited recently, donating the organs of a family member who has just suffered brain death is almost non-existent. In the past 12 years there have been fewer than 150 liver transplants, fewer than 40 heart transplants and only two lung transplants. This puts India down among the very lowest donation rates in the world. So tiny is the flow of organs from deceased patients that in a country with a population of one billion there are only seven full-time and sixty part-time transplant surgeons.

Just about the only organ donations that take place are from living donors who give one of their kidneys to a family member. Generally, both the donor and the recipient recover well and can go on to live virtually normal lives. Such individual acts of courage, however, cannot touch the main problem and the consequences in lives lost are massive. Yet transplantation is one of the triumphs of modern medicine, an everyday operation in hospitals all over the world.

Just how much of a triumph was illustrated by an extraordinary event that took place recently in Ludhiana: the All-India Transplant Games and South Asia Transplant Olympics, organized by a team from the Dayanand Medical College and Hospital, led and inspired by Professor B.S. Aulakh. "We wanted to show that transplantation does not simply prolong life," he says. "Instead it gives terminally-ill patients a new life."

More than a hundred competitors from Bangladesh, Nepal, Pakistan and Sri Lanka, as well as India, some of them recipients, others kidney donors, ran, jumped, swam, played badminton and threw javelins with a verve that made them indistinguishable from people who have never been sick at all.

The middle-aged ladies, most of whom ran in their street clothes, were particularly impressive. Scarves flying, wide trousers flapping and saris billowing, they seemed the symbol of the new India: beneficiaries of cutting edge medical technology allied to liberation from traditional taboos.

After the games, on with the hiking boots and into the Himalayas (with son Michael, who took the photo.) This is Pangong Lake at 14,000 ft., where there is no one to stop you walking wherever you want. Where, in fact, there is no one at all.

Many contestants were over 55. One was 67. Another, a 32 year-old from Pakistan, who had received a kidney from his mother 10 years ago, competed in no fewer than six events. Age for age, the participants were more like athletes than the normal population, helped by the better diet and exercise their doctors insist on.

As everywhere, their stories are full of unexpected twists that can spell the difference between life and death. One 33 year-old woman, whose kidneys were failing a year ago, was comforted at the time by her sister saying she would donate one of hers if it became necessary. But when the time came the sister said she couldn't go through with it. "At that moment I saw in my wife's eyes the thought 'I'm going to die,' " her husband told me.

Instead, he checked with his doctors, found that his kidneys were compatible with hers and donated one of them to her. Ten days after the operation he was back at work and says neither he nor his wife has ever had a significant problem since then.

A happy boy of eight demonstrated another of the astonishing developments of transplantation techniques. He had received a part of his mother's liver, which has since grown inside him to the size needed for his young body, and will go on growing as he matures, while the part left in his mother's body has also grown to the size she needs. Throughout the games both mother and son beamed at each other with the contentment that comes with glowing health and mutual admiration.

But, because of the negligible donation rates from the brain dead, which are the dominant source of organs in Western countries, these people are the rare exceptions in India. Grinding day-after-day poverty and the illiteracy, superstition and fear that go with it look like being an insurmountable barrier to making any dent in the problem among huge sections of the population for the foreseeable future.

Taking out the organs of a loved one, even though it is treated with all the carefulness of a normal surgical operation, is also for many Indians too horrifying to contemplate. They say no and in effect sign the death warrant of three or four other people.

The hope of narrowing the gap has to lie with the rapidly-expanding middle class who, with all their problems, might in time come to recognize that faced with a situation in which their own loved one cannot be saved, they can shield other families from the devastation they themselves are going through.

First published in The Times of India 2007

This is the kind of vehicle I envisaged having to be brought in to dig up our drain. Worse: this one has run off the fire road and is hanging over a 200 ft. drop. Would they charge us extra for hauling it back? I wondered.

Unhappy Holidays

For everything, they say, there is a season. A time to weep and a time to laugh, etc. The season your household doesn't want, however, is to have a blocked drain between Christmas and New Year. As you can tell, I speak in the season for bitterness.

It started with a phone call to a plumber after Christmas Day and being told the next appointments were being scheduled in six days. I managed to whittle that down to three but the time passed in a mixture of frustration, inconvenience and self-pity.

When the plumbing season arrived at last, so did the plumber and he was reassuring. "Don't worry, Mr. Green, I'm going to take care of you."

But the snake he had wasn't long enough and whatever extra help was needed wouldn't be available until after the weekend. More frustration, increased pain and unprecedented self-pity.

When the new snake arrived, it was long enough but was coming up against an obstacle too stubborn for it to deal with. The new diagnosis: things were worse than expected. In fact, things were much worse than expected. "We may have to dig up your driveway," they warned. I foresaw weeks more of bathing in teaspoonfuls of water.

Eventually a whole team arrived with a snake attached to a camera — a marvelous leap of technology, being able to see what Harry Lime had to go into the sewers of Vienna in person to see — and a drill with teeth like Tyrannosaurus Rex. The pictures were fascinating but upsetting: thick tree roots growing lustily in a fast-flowing river, an underwater jungle.

"Don't worry, Mr. Green, we're going to take care of you," they said. For more authoritative comfort, my thoughts went back to Ecclesiastes: "There is a season to plant and a season to uproot."

An hour later the team leader came back. "I have some good news," he said. "We can see where the blockage is." But if some good news comes, can much bigger bad news be far behind? Yes, here it came.

"The blockage is just where your pipe meets the main drain. So, if we can't drill it out, the county will have to dig up the street." "How much will that cost?" "Poof," he sighed, his shrug and outstretched hands suggesting it could be in the millions. "But we're going to try to take care of you."

Going to *try.* I went indoors and checked how much money was in my IRA.

An hour more and, miraculously, it was done. The drill had demolished the subterranean forest. The dishwasher washed, toilets flushed cheerfully, socks didn't have to be washed by hand.

When the head man handed me an invoice bringing the total to $2,400, I almost kissed him with relief and we all parted on the best of terms. Since then I have been thrusting from my mind the thought that the idea that the road would have to be dug up was simply dreamed up to make the bill seem low.

Instead I have found consolation elsewhere, remembering the story of a Russian who ordered a car and was told it would be delivered in 10 years. "OK," he said, "but please come in the morning." Why the morning? the salesman asked. "The plumber is coming that afternoon," he explained.

IN THE HIGH MOUNTAINS, SUDDENLY IT'S FALL

Fall has arrived in the local mountains with startling suddenness. Two weeks ago I took a leisurely hike along the backbone of the San Gabriel Mountains, sunning myself from time to time on the hot rocks, the desert haze on one side, the ocean haze on the other.

The bear that crossed my path moments earlier, and seemed to be ambling along, moved so fast that he disappeared into the undergrowth before I could get the camera out of my pocket. A useful lesson: don't try to outrun them. Climbing a tree is probably not a good idea either. Maybe my method was best after all.

This week, at 9,000 feet, I had to walk warily around patches of hard ice. To the south, fleecy autumnal clouds were building up over the ocean. To the north the desert air was scrubbed clean enough to see clearly the growth of habitation in what used to be the dreaded empty Mojave. The sky was deep blue and the bright red leaves of the one deciduous tree I remember seemed too much of a showoff for these subdued surroundings.

I started early and saw the full moon go down and the sun come up. A cool breeze made me shiver as I took the first steps on the trail but soon the wind died down and complete stillness among the trees blanketed everything, like being in an empty concert hall.

I walked past the place where, a two weeks before, a well-fed bear lumbered across the trail just ahead of me and disappeared into the vegetation. I have often asked myself what I would do if I met one at close quarters. Now I know. I would stand stock still, trying to look like a Jeffrey pine, while Red Skelton's immortal verse flashed through my mind:

Algie saw the bear, the bear saw Algie.
The bear was bulgy, the bulge was Algie.

But my bear moved on without a glance and, with the turn in the weather, I imagine he is now thinking "Half-past November already. Time for a few months' nap." At any rate, I didn't see him again or any of the squirrels that were scampering so eagerly last time or even any little sunbathing lizards. All around the tempo of life was visibly slowing.

In those three or four hours, I didn't see any human life either. I'd guess that fewer than 0.1 percent of all those nearby millions ever take to these trails. To all the rest, this kind of pastime has little appeal: it's boring or uncomfortable or just a waste of time with hard labor thrown in. And, course, they all have competing interests. I understand their reluctance: it's a different world. But what an experience they are missing.

The Creature on the Trail

Do you remember the origin of Catch-22? In Joseph Heller's World War II masterpiece it's when, by strictly following the rules to solve a problem, every door but one closes and that one leads you back to the original problem.

Thus Doc Daneeka turns down Yossarian's plan to plead insanity so as to be excused from flying dangerous missions. "You mean there's a catch?" Yossarian asks. "Sure there's a catch," Doc explains: anyone who wants to be excused from flying dangerous missions can't be insane. If you have had a disagreement with the IRS you will know the feeling but I had an experience recently without any help from the government.

One morning very early I set out on a hike through the forest. It was a perfect day, black as night so to speak, warm, not a breath of air and or a sound. As I walked on, however, I heard the noise of an animal ahead, a deep-pitched, insistent moaning sound which became louder and more frequent as I moved toward a small clump of trees.

As I understand it, animals make these repeated sounds either to keep out intruders who they think are ugly or to invite intruders in who they think are beautiful. Wanting neither to fight nor couple with this stranger, I began to have qualms about confronting it. The basic rule is that, if it feels unsafe and you are alone, go back.

I tried to stiffen up my sinews, as Henry V advised in somewhat similar circumstances. "Are you a man or a mouse?" I asked myself but only Bob Hope's response came to mind when he was asked the same question: "Throw down a piece of cheese and you'll find out." But I imagined the humiliation of my weeping family having to rouse the firefighters to rescue an old fool last seen being carried off in the jaws of a lovesick mountain lion.

I stood there in the dark, torn between going on and doing what I find so painful, turning back. In the end I was sensible. I turned round -- and regretted it immediately, so much in fact that I went back the next morning at the same time but saw nothing.

That afternoon, however, another hiker who I'd confessed my cowardice to emailed me to say he had gone out too and had not only heard but seen the creature – not a mournful jackal or a wailing banshee or a lonely orangutan that had escaped from the zoo, but an owl.

Now, as we know from Thomas Gray's *Elegy*, the owl does no more than 'gently mope' when some human disturbs its peace. So I could have walked on as a man without the slightest problem. But, by turning back and becoming a mouse, an owl's favorite breakfast, my chances of surviving, if seen, would have been close to nil.

Clearly this conundrum is not in the same league as Yossarian's. Nevertheless, it is not good for the ego.

I'm not afraid of this one.

I feel also I could have regained some lost ground when my hiker friend broke the news. I could have said what the English schoolboy said when told the same thing. "Yes, I know it was an 'owl. But 'oo 'owled?"

I Meet One of the World's Most Beautiful Women and Receive a Surprisingly Passionate Response

In a small restaurant in Rome a few months ago our table was next to that of a singularly beautiful woman, vaguely familiar. "She's a television personality," my friend, Andrea, told me, "and is sensitive to human issues." It was Alessia Marcuzzi, whose weekly show "Big Brother," sends the pulse of every red-blooded male viewer in Italy racing – and most anemic ones too.

Well, I have a good cause also so, when we got up to leave, I excused myself for interrupting her talk with her handsome companion and introduced myself as Nicholas Green's father. Nicholas was killed twenty years before but I was sure she would remember. I don't think I have ever met an Italian who was a teenager or older at the time who didn't remember. In any event, she did, said some kind things and we left.

That night, however, she put an item about our meeting on her Facebook page. By the next day 30,000 people had said they 'liked' it. Seven hundred of them sent in a comment, most of them expressing passionate support for organ donation, and 1,600 thought the story was worth putting on their own Facebooks, potentially reaching hundreds of thousands more. Postings on the site around that time were averaging about one thousand 'likes.'

"Here she is, Maggie. I hope you two will be great friends."
Credit Courtesy Vanity Fair Italia/photo Sylvie Lancrenon

So, yes, it's true, we all know it, organ donation is normally too remote a subject to be of much interest generally. Time and again, however, I have seen that once people feel a personal connection or see a sympathetic human face in it, organ donation can become riveting.

This is not surprising: every one of us could need a new heart or kidney or liver at any time -- or tissue to relieve chronic pain, such as skin to cure excruciating burns or bone to straighten spines. Equally, any of us could be an organ or tissue donor. Add in that transplantation is also a story of life coming out of death and how can it not compel attention when people recognize what is at stake?

Some have no choice about being interested: they are on a long and lengthening waiting list, waking up every day thankful that they are still alive but with growing anxiety as they wait for a gift from someone they can't even visualize.

It is an agonizing wait, made worse by them being completely helpless to speed up the process. Every time the telephone rings -- or the buzzer they carry with them wherever they are goes off -- their hopes soar. Every time it is not the call they want, they slump back to the interminable wait.

The overwhelming majority of people in most developed countries say they are in favor of organ donation. Yet donated organs are scarce everywhere. Partly this is because demand has increased so rapidly, as physicians have found ever more cases where a transplant is the preferred, often the only, cure.

But it is also because the setting is so forbidding. Families faced with the decision become aware that, at the moment they say 'yes,' they are also saying goodbye. No more clinging to hopes of a miraculous recovery or fantasies of setting off on a favorite walk together.

There are also many twists of the knife. On Nicholas' last day I went into the small room to see him one more time and my heart leapt: there he was in bed, breathing regularly, his chest gently rising and falling.

"He's getting better," I thought excitedly. "I must tell someone right away." And then a split-second later the crash to earth as I realized it was simply a clever machine breathing for him.

He never regained consciousness. I can still see quite clearly the doctors in that sunlit room in Messina saying gently to us, "We have bad news for you. We can find no brain activity." We sat there, holding hands, not talking.

I tried to absorb the thought that I would never again meet him coming home from school or hear him say "Goodnight, daddy." Then Maggie, thoughtful as always, said quietly, "Now that he's gone, shouldn't we donate the organs?"

For the first time since he was shot, there was a glimmer of light in the blackness. Something good could come out of this mindless violence after all. I said "yes" and that's all there was to it. We told the doctors and went back to the hotel to pack. It could not have been simpler.

Of course, it doesn't take the pain away: after twenty years I still think of Nicholas several times a day and always with a sense of an irreparable loss. But it has put something on the other side of the balance.

Thousands of other families make the same decision each year but, though it was as clear to them as it was to us, for many others it is much harder and made harder still because brain death is sudden death. They have no preparation for it and arrive at the hospital to find someone they love who was in perfect health a few hours before is now dead or dying.

They may be too confused or too distraught to understand the options. Often there are complications. Perhaps a child was hit by a car when running across the road because of what one parent considers the other's carelessness. Perhaps there has been a bitter divorce and the two sides now have to discuss a deeply personal subject neither of them has ever given any serious thought to.

Perhaps just one family member is adamantly opposed and, at a time like this, the rest are unwilling to argue. There is no time to deliberate: the decision must be made there or then or not at all. And so, many families, who in calmer moments would have thought of all the good they could do by agreeing, instead find themselves saying no.

The results of transplantation differ according to which organ it is but in the United States 90 percent of heart recipients are alive one year after the operation, 75 percent after five years and 55 percent after ten. Given that all these people were very sick, that some were on the threshold of death, and that some will die of unrelated causes, it is an amazing record.

Oh, and by the way, speaking to beautiful strangers in restaurants can also produce surprisingly good results.

First published in the Italian Journal of Cardiology.

Don't they ever learn? (Photo Hotshot Imaging Inc.)

Temptation? Give Into It. But Only Once

This past summer I narrowly escaped becoming a pervert. Even at 82, that's not easy.

I owe my deliverance to an observation by Voltaire, who argued that to perform some disgraceful act once can be seen as a search for knowledge and therefore an honorable intellectual pursuit but, if it becomes a habit, is inevitably corrupting. Or, as he put it succinctly, "Once, a philosopher; twice, a pervert."

The temptation: do again what I did a year earlier with my children and grandchildren: raft on the Middle Fork of the American River, rightly billed as one of California's most thrilling adventures open to the layman. The salvation: I refused to go despite the man-or-mouse question hanging heavily in the air. Whatever the answer to that, I told myself, I'm at least smart enough to know I'm not an amphibian.

The trip starts, remember, by shooting at the speed of a bullet through a tunnel, unique in rafting, blasted by gold miners to divert the river, the raft careening like a wild thing, the boiling white water glowing in the nightmarish semi-darkness.

A series of Class 3 rapids quickly follows, defined as "intense and powerful" and "requiring complex maneuvers" in which the raft twists, turns, bounces and spins and can flip over. If that is not enough, there are also some Class 4s, a terrifying turn of the screw. Falling out of the boat is described as "unusual but not all that rare" and photographs of past trips displayed by the outfitting companies show spectacular examples.

We all survived that earlier trip, said afterward that it wasn't so dangerous after all and gave silent thanks for the expertise of the river guide who sits in the back of the boat and does all the real work.

This year the younger family members wanted to do it again but, with Voltaire whispering in my ear, a compromise was reached: we would do the tamer south fork of the river, which nevertheless has a string of Class 3 rapids, whose character can be inferred from their names: Triple Threat, Corkscrew and Meatgrinder.

All went well, however, and I have to admit there is a unique thrill in floating placidly down a flat stretch of a sparkling river in a majestic canyon and hearing in the distance a whisper, turning into a drone, then into a roar, the current quickening and, ahead, madly bouncing waves, then a whoosh as you top the rapid, rocks everywhere except for an absurdly narrow and zigzagging channel of churning water that you are going to have to find your way through, the boat gyrating and shuddering, then magically finding that you are shooting through the gap, and the sudden relief: "Well, we made that one."

So, though I plan next year to spend my vacation days in the nearby Sierra Nevada mountains, taking contemplative hikes, where the only water is in the plastic bottle, I have fond memories of the liquid version of Mr. Toad's Wild Ride.

Put me down as a recovering pervert.

First published in The Sacramento Bee

GOODBYE GLOOM

You would think the recent succession of grey mornings would be a signal to the few hikers who go out early to pull the bedclothes back over their heads. Instead they provide some of the most satisfying views of the year.

It's true that, when you drive to a trailhead along the Angeles Crest Highway, your mood often reflects the gloom. Mostly, you are on your own on an eerily empty road but, peering through the mist, from time to time you see coming toward you a car, then another right behind it, and another, a string of them, headlights on – five, ten, sometimes fifteen at a time -- bumper to bumper.

Silvery now but soon changing to pink, then orange, then gold – but from underneath just a grey day.

Since the places to overtake are few and far between on this winding, two-lane road, and there is scarcely a building for forty miles, presumably they have kept in that formation, staring at the same license plate in front of them, all the way from Palmdale. The string disappears into the mist and you are alone again.

But then a wonderful thing happens. In the space of a couple of hundred yards the mist thins and disappears and in front of you the whole bowl of mountains is bathed in sunlight. That point marks the very end of the gloom.

You can look back and see the clouds surging up the valley but here, even at that time of day, the sun is warm, the sky perfectly clear. Or, as Robert Browning put it on just such a day, "God's in his Heaven, All's right with the world." And for a while it certainly seems so.

The trailhead is right there and, after not much more than a half an hour of walking, surrounded by sunlit peaks, you come to the first long view south. On some days the entire view below you, from east to west, and over the ocean, is covered in fleecy clouds -- depressing when seen from below (even the fish are snuggled under their bedclothes) but gold-streaked gossamer from above.

In the far distance a few peaks or Catalina Island may stick out – more magic. On less cloudy days the mist, blown about by a soft breeze, makes swift-changing patterns – the 5000 block of La Cañada Boulevard, maybe, socked in, the 3000 block in clear sunshine, the first family saying "When is this dreary weather going to end?" and the second "Don't forget the sunscreen."

To an outsider my steady but slow hike may look like a ponderous, perhaps wearisome, way to start the day but inside I am re-living the liberation that being high up and alone in the mountains always brings.

Leaving No Trace

Did you see the story of the oil-rich sheikh who has had his name bulldozed in the sand in such massive letters that they can be seen from outer space? Let's hope they spelled it right. That would be a costly typo.

Obviously, unlike us, he wasn't made to read "Ozymandias" at high school. If he had he would have remembered Shelley's description of the traveler who came across a vast monument in the desert with its disdainful inscription: "Look on my works, ye Mighty, and despair!" but which was now in total ruin.

"Nothing beside remains. Round the decay
Of that colossal wreck, boundless and bare
The lone and level sands stretch far away."

Lacking that information, however, the sheikh could instead have put on his boots, gone out on the Mt. Lukens fire road and received the same lesson.

In the last week or two, however early I start, I have seen the footprints of another hiker. I'm there by 6 o'clock and, with no other car in the small parking lot, I know he is not ahead and so was the last one there the evening before.

Even in this empty place, these marks go as quickly as they came, erased by the handful of bikers or a rare truck servicing the antennae at the summit. Search as I might, when I go up in the mornings, I can find only an occasional sign of the footprints I made the day before.

From time to time, determined to make a statement similar to Sheikh Hamad's, I step off the road at one of the hairpin bends and plant my boot hard into the deep dust at the edges. By next day, however, even those signs have largely disappeared. It isn't easy to become immortal.

Man Friday's boots are a couple of sizes bigger than mine and with pointy toes so I know something about him. Like me, he prefers to go at a time when the solitariness won't be disturbed by meeting even one other person. He strides ahead purposefully, rarely straying to the side to stop and look at the view. I also see the prints of a dog, though I don't know if the two travel together or if the dog hikes every evening alone too.

If I had Sherlock Holmes' powers of observation, I might be able to work out other things, such as whether he shops at Trader Joe's or Ralphs, but for now I just enjoy the feeling of sharing in a common pleasure. It's just another of the little gifts that living next to this massive open area brings.

My usual morning hike starts down there, near where the car is parked: a three-mile roundtrip with a gain of 600 ft.

Once upon a time, when I was a young reporter in England, I did think I might make a more enduring mark. Running to catch a train one day, I suddenly realized that the sidewalk ahead had just been covered in hot asphalt. Swerving at the last moment to avoid it, I managed to step with my right foot into the road but my left sank momentarily into the gooey surface.

For the next ten years, whenever I went that way I was pleased to see that my mark was still there, like that of a pterodactyl in a primeval swamp, and wondered whether future archaeologists might puzzle over this one-legged species that walked on its toes. When eventually the sidewalk was replaced as part of the central city's redevelopment I felt as though a little bit of me had been redeveloped too.

To which my wife said, "It's about time."

The Cowboy on the Hill

It was soon after dawn on the San Rafael Hills, a dozen miles or so north of Los Angeles, and I was on my own, when I saw looming out of the thick mist a lone figure. For some reason I associated him with trouble. Luckily his back was towards me and for a split-second I wondered whether to avoid getting too close.

By then, however, I had realized it wasn't a man at all, but a cutout figure of one. But not just any man. A long, lean, dangerous man. And not just any long, lean, dangerous man but Clint Eastwood. And he was in a smoldering pose made famous by "A Fistful of Dollars."

He stood there on the crest of a hill overlooking the steep-sided valley through which the Glendale Freeway runs and ready at the drop of his famous hat to ride into the quiet township below and root out the corroding vice behind that all-too-respectable façade.

As usual he made his own law, a cigar in his mouth despite the clear prohibition of smoking at the trailhead and no sign of a poop scoop for his horse. In the weeks that followed the silhouette became a welcoming feature of the drive home for thousands of commuters on the freeway.

Then one day, a few weeks ago, I took the same hike and on the last few steps saw the figure had gone. Instead, on his knees, was a man trying to put the pieces together of something that had obviously been brutally vandalized.

He turned out to be the artist, whose first name is Justin and likes to be known only by that name. We chatted sadly for a while and I told him of another work, now almost part of me, that has the same goal of making outdoor art an integral part of everyday life.

This is the Children's Bell Tower in Bodega Bay, north of San Francisco, where we lived for many years and which was suggested to us by Bruce Hasson, a San Francisco sculptor, after our son Nicholas was killed. Bruce's idea was to allow anyone, who wanted to remember a child, to send in a bell.

The media took up the idea and the Italian weekly magazine, Oggi, which had always followed our story closely, even set up a collection point. Almost immediately offers of bells started to arrive: school bells, ships' bells, mining bells, cow bells, some specially made, some that had been in the family for generations, in the end 140 of them.

Most of them are from Italy though, while there was still some space, when someone with a poignant story from somewhere else came to us, among them Japan and Paraguay, we tried to add their bell. The centerpiece is a magnificent bell, with Nicholas' name and that of his seven recipients on it, specially cast by the foundry that has been making bells for the papacy for a thousand years, and was blessed by Pope John Paul II, who was very touched by the story.

Photo by Martin Green

Without ever taking a penny for his time Bruce designed, built and maintains the tower which is in a place of wild beauty, an open windswept area behind the coastal dunes. I think of it as a little piece of Italy's soul by the Pacific Ocean.

When I described it, Justin loved the idea too and one day he wrote to me saying that he had repaired the cutout but with a small difference. The next morning, again early and again on a day thick with mist, I went to see it and my heart leapt. Clint's right arm was now outstretched and in his hand was a bell.

A plaque on his back invited anyone who went there to ring the bell and commit to becoming an organ donor. In the last 18 years tears have come to my eyes many times but I have rarely sobbed. I did that day, however, when I rang the bell and thought how proud our gentle, thoughtful Nicholas would have been to be part of bringing people together in such an all-enveloping way.

Another week or two passed and I took the trail again. Clint had disappeared and this time there was no trace of any pieces. No one seems to know what happened.

But before it went this simple cutout had left a message: in one stroke a figure that had at first looked like a threat, then pure destructiveness, had become a symbol of hope. It also left an invaluable lesson: at every moment of the day we all have choices.

First published in Update, magazine of the United Network for Organ Sharing.

Unequal contest: the rat (in the shadow) is still alive but only just.

Death as a Fact of Life

A truck on a fire road close to home passed me, nice and slowly, to keep down the cloud of dust. A hundred yards ahead it stopped, the driver and passenger got out and stood by the side of the road.

"Be careful," they shouted. "There's a rattlesnake here."

I walked up and saw not just a snake but a few inches away a rat lying on its side. "It's alive," I said, more to myself than anyone else. It had looked so dead but then I saw its ear twitch and a tremble going the length of its body. The snake slithered nearer, its fangs shot out and the rat jumped nearly a foot, as though it had touched a live wire, shuddered horribly and then lay still.

The snake wound its way unhurriedly to a gap in the rocks by the roadside. "It'll be back later for dinner," the driver commented, and we all moved on.

Twenty minutes later I had finished my hike and was back at the same place. By now the rat was lying on the other side of the road, three or four feet from where I first saw it, and the snake was the same few inches away from it.

I saw a slight movement. "It's still alive," I said out loud, though this time there was no one to hear.

The snake moved closer, cautious as ever, and struck again. Again the rat, convulsed, shot forward, though not as far this time, and lay there, huddled in the fetal position, praying to all the gods it worships to be left alone to sleep.

Once more the snake drew back, waited and then moved in, more self-assured this time and its victim's response now was just the slightest quiver.

The snake went back to its hiding place, leaving what had been a nervous system of unimaginably complex connections and sensitivity lying in the middle of the road as unfeeling as the rocks around it.

The next morning there wasn't a sign of anything unusual. Why would there be? Within a few miles of that death there are — what would you say? — millions of others every day: ants, flies, gnats, butterflies, birds, squirrels, deer, everything that lives there; and all their deaths in one way or another helping keep something else alive.

In the urbane salons of the 18th century, there was a famous joke about it:

"Great fleas have little fleas upon their backs to bite 'em
And little fleas have lesser fleas and so ad infinitum."

So, yes, death is a commonplace thing — the most certain of all the facts of life — though that doesn't make that tiny step from high-strung liveliness to annihilation any less shocking. But it also carries a useful lesson, a reminder that, when taking sides on any issue, there is always another point of view.

First published in the La Cañada Valley Sun

I Hear a World-Famous Lawyer, Who Doesn't Exist, Snubbing Me Publicly: Am I Going Crazy?

"Rumpole, your nose is always buried in The Times at breakfast time," I heard Hilda's scolding voice say on the car radio. And the usual bored, irritated response from her husband, Horace: "I'm reading the obituary of Cole Porter," he managed to grind out. "Well, I'm reading something in the Daily Telegraph much more interesting than dead American songwriters," Hilda responded. (I'm paraphrasing, but this is the gist).

For the hundredth time I wondered how Rumpole, brilliant lawyer, wit and scourge of the pretentious and cretinous, could have married such a combination of harpy and ignoramus. (A naive question. John Mortimer created her so Horace could pour scorn on someone so unremittingly unappetizing that all our sympathies would be with him — and by implication Mortimer himself. All writers have little tricks to put themselves in a favorable light: that's why we write.)

I also wondered for the thousandth time about coincidence. I never listen to the radio and yet here I was in England, having just switched on to hear the latest news and there were Mortimer's iconic characters — people who never existed — discussing me. Or, rather, pointedly ignoring me. Yes, me.

You see, years before I had written Cole Porter's obituary for the London Daily Telegraph and it was published on the very day Mortimer had chosen for his story. It was another of life's blows to learn that it never occurred to either of them that the article that I had labored over so painstakingly, and of which I was secretly so proud, was worth a glance. He disdained the Telegraph, she disdained the obituaries in it.

It is possible, of course, the Fates had guided me to that program as a reminder that, as Robert Burns has shown, how far we all are from seeing ourselves as others see us. The fact that Burns chose a louse to illustrate this human failing didn't help.

But then again, as Michael, my oldest son, a physicist, points out, "There are billions and billions of things happening all the time. Some of them are bound to match." I agree with that. It's the rational explanation.

Still, these matches are sometimes a little uncanny. I was on my way home from Italy, where I had given a series of talks involving another of my sons, Nicholas, who, as you will know by now, had become an iconic figure himself there.

One evening in Brindisi I was having dinner with two friends, Luigi and Teresa, when her cellphone rang. It was her brother. "I'm with Luigi and a visitor from the United States, Reg Green," she told him.

The Greens and organ recipients meet. Standing, left to right: Reg; Maggie; Andrea Mongiardo, recipient of Nicholas' heart; Francesco Mondello, cornea recipient; Tino Motta, kidney recipient; Anna Maria Di Ceglie, kidney recipient; Eleanor. Seated, left to right: Laura; Maria Pia Pedalà, liver recipient; Domenica Galletta, cornea recipient; Silvia Ciampi, pancreas recipient; Martin.

All seven of Nicholas' recipients plus five Greens (1996)
(Courtesy of Oggi Magazine, Italy)

There was a slight pause, then he replied, "Please tell him I was one of the crew of the air force plane that took Nicholas' body home to America."

Looking Down on Los Angeles

"So you live in California," they say, their eyes aglow. "Where?" "Los Angeles," you say. Their faces fall. They'd hoped for Sausalito or Pebble Beach.

Now in their minds' eye, these people see flat, seemingly endless streets, with tacky stores, petering out at seedy beaches. You stiffen because, after all, there is truth in it.

But let me give you a different picture. We are standing at the top of Mt.Lowe, 5,600 ft. up, far above the planes we can see coming into the airport. The trailhead where we started is less than an hour's drive to downtown. In front of us are the entire Los Angeles basin and the mountains flanking it.

At that moment, one of my 17-year old children is getting ready to go to one of the places down there, the Hollywood Bowl which, when I first saw it in a Frank Sinatra film and impossibly far away, seemed to me to have all the grandeur of its ancestors in ancient Greece and has lost none of it appeal on closer acquaintance.

The other twin is scuba diving off Catalina Island, also clearly visible. There too is a classical parallel, a version of Capri, which the Roman Emperor, Tiberius, chose as the best place in the whole empire to live when he went into voluntary exile. And, just like Capri, it is set like a jewel in an azure sea.

Down there also, in Hollywood, is my wife who, benefiting from the singing and acting talent that floods into this area from every country in the world, is a costumer for a small opera company and is buying fabrics and costumes at bargain prices, like the pants worn by Jack Nicholson in Batman for $3 in an auction.

Behind us is total wilderness, chaparral-covered slopes steeper than the angle of repose and virtually impossible to move across except on the one through road we came in on and a few dirt roads and trails. The land is so dry that only the toughest vegetation can survive but within sight, for months of the year, there is enough snow on Mt. Baldy to support a ski center.

Mt. Wilson, a couple of miles away, whose telescope once could peer more deeply into space than any other, has been overtaken as a pioneer but, instead, the Jet Propulsion Lab in the valley below is now the cutting edge that has made the surface of Mars a reality to everyone in the world who has a television set.

Down there too are the public schools that three of my children attended, whose stature is summed up by a comment by Ms. Baldwin, a middle school teacher, who told parents at a back-to-school night: "At the end of this course your children *will* like Shakespeare. Money back guaranteed," which I think of as the most satisfying comment I have ever heard from any teacher.

Mt. Lowe country. "Is this Los Angeles, Daddy?" (Photo: Bryan Stewart)

To the left in the distance is the desert with the mountains above it standing out dramatically in the dry air. To the right – also only an hour or so from downtown – is another mountain chain whose interior is so remote that it was chosen as a haven to bring back the condor, only thirty of which were then living in the whole of North America.

None of the other largest cities in the world comes anywhere near to this variety of experience. It's hard to resist the paraphrase: "Whoever is tired of Los Angeles is tired of life."

(First published in the Los Angeles Times)

EVENSONG

It isn't *all* hiking, of course. When Maggie, the costumer for the Pacific Opera Project, is out of town, I occasionally invite the chorus over for a musical evening.